BASTOGNE
ARDENNES 1944

Steven Smith and Simon Forty

Casemate
PHILADELPHIA & OXFORD

Published in the United States of America and Great Britain in 2016
by CASEMATE PUBLISHERS
1950 Lawrence Road, Havertown, PA 19083
and 10 Hythe Bridge Street, Oxford, OX1 2EW

ISBN-13: 978-1-61200-434-1

Produced by Greene Media Ltd.

Cataloging-in-publication data is available from the Library of Congress
and the British Library.

10 9 8 7 6 5 4 3 2 1

Printed and bound in China
For a complete list of Casemate titles please contact:
CASEMATE PUBLISHERS (US)
Telephone (610) 853-9131, Fax (610) 853-9146
E-mail: casemate@casematepublishers.com

CASEMATE PUBLISHERS (UK)
Telephone (01865) 241249, Fax (01865) 794449
E-mail: casemate-uk@casematepublishers.co.uk

Acknowledgments
Most of the photos are US Signal Corps images that have come from a
number of sources. Grateful thanks go to BattlefieldHistorian.com, NARA
College Park, MD, and the George Forty Library for historic photos; other
credits are noted on the photographs—WikiCommons has proved
extremely useful. If anyone is missing or incorrectly credited, apologies:
please notify the authors through the publishers.

I'd like to thank in particular Tom Timmermans and Battledetective.com for
the Then and Nows. Other thanks are due to Leo Marriott, Peter Hendrikx,
Barry van Veen of STIWOT, Mark Franklin (maps), Ian Hughes (design)
Richard Wood and the military cyclists (particularly Peter Anderson) for photos
and enthusiasm.

Previous page:
The 101st Airborne monument at the Mardasson Memorial. *Peter Anderson*

This Page:
11th Armored Division entered the war late, arriving in France on
December 16. It reached Neufchâteau on the 29th, two days before
this photo was taken, attacking north toward Houffalize.

Above:
26 battlefield markers identify the
extent of German incursions into the
Ardennes. This one is at Foy Notre
Dame, north of Celles. Around
Bastogne there are markers at Foy and
Longchamps.

Contents

Introduction

BY SEPTEMBER OF 1944, the Allies had every right to expect that the war against Germany would be over by Christmas. The Anglo-Americans, after their breakout at Normandy, and the Soviets, after their destruction of German Army Group Center, had advanced literally hundreds of miles that summer against a once-mighty Wehrmacht that had been largely obliterated, with the rest of its units in headlong retreat.

However, Hitler's armies did hold on to basic military arithmetic. Their conquests had been so vast—from the Atlantic seaboard to the depths of European Russia—that they had plenty of space to work with. And when the Allies rapidly traversed that space themselves it was clear they would outrun their logistical networks, even as the German supply lines shortened. Combined with the difficult northern European weather that set in during fall, gaining interior lines, and German persistence in denying the Allies use of coastal ports, the fronts stabilized, with Hitler's divisions able to rebuild and resupply quicker than the Allies could. The worm was about to turn.

After the failure of Montgomery's daring airborne invasion in Holland, Operation Market Garden, the Western Allies' front congealed basically along the German border, as the U.S. First, Third, and Ninth armies hammered their heads against the Westwall, primarily at Aachen and Metz. In between was the forest region of the Ardennes, which the Americans considered a quiet sector, into which they sent new divisions to be acclimated, and battered veteran divisions to rest and recuperate. For an 80-mile stretch, roughly from Monschau in the north to Echternach in the south, the front was held by only four U.S. infantry divisions, two of them green and two of them battered, with one raw armored division in reserve. As his strength renewed, Hitler decided to launch a surprise counteroffensive through the Ardennes.

Since the Germans had also used the Ardennes as an invasion route in 1870, 1914, and most spectacularly in 1940, one is entitled to wonder why the Allies neglected that sector at the end of 1944. The answer is that they simply could not envision the recuperative powers of the German armed forces. Believing the estimates of their bomber chiefs, they had no idea that German industry had actually reached a peak of production by fall 1944; that the Wehrmacht still retained sufficient fuel stocks; and that many of the frontline divisions reported "destroyed" in Normandy were still intact, only needing new replacements and equipment.

For their counteroffensive the Germans prepared two powerful armies, the Sixth SS Panzer under Sepp Dietrich and the Fifth Panzer under Hasso von Manteuffel. With flank support the attacking force would amount to 30 divisions. The objective was to crash through the thin front in the Ardennes and then hook north across the Meuse River toward Antwerp, thereby cutting off U.S. First Army and Montgomery's entire 21st Army Group. The Allied front would be split in half—a war-winning blow.

In the event, Sixth SS Panzer Army was unable to even reach the Meuse; the true schwerpunkt of the attack would switch to Fifth Panzer Army, which drove a 60-mile "bulge" into the U.S. front. However, the road net in the southern sector was dominated by the town of Bastogne, which the Germans surrounded but were unable to conquer. The gallant U.S. defense of Bastogne would turn out to be the key to the battle.

Oosterhout

Dorsten

Breda

Roosendaal

Gelderkirchen

Tilburg

NETHERLANDS

Geldern

Bergen op Zoom

**Allied Front Line
16 December 1944**

Essen

Moers

Helmond

Eindhoven

Venlo

Krefeld

Antwerp Canal

Düsseldorf

Maas R.

Niers R.

Rhine R.

Antwerp

Roermond

Schelde R.

Lier

Albert Canal

München-
Gladbach

Rur R.

Erft R.

Mechelen

van Willebroek

Köln

Hasselt

Heerlen

Jülich

GERMANY

Leuven

Eschweiler

Düren

Tienen

Aachen

Erft R.

Brussels

Tongeren

Sennette R.

Wavre

Block line

Euskirchen

21
XXXXX
12

BELGIUM

Liege

Meuse R.

Verviers

Huy

Spa

Ourthe R.

Malmedy

XXXX
FIFTEENTH
Zangen

Louviere

Sambre R.

Namur

Stavelot

Charleroi

Châtelet

St. Vith

XXXX
SIXTH
Dietrich

Beaumont

Dinant

Marche

La Roche

XXXXX
B
Model

Houffalize

Rocheort

Cleff R.

XXXX
FIFTH
Manteuffel

Block line

St. Hubert

Bastogne

Lesse R.

XXXX
SEVENTH
Brandenburger

Süre R.

Our R.

Bouillon

Semois R.

Echternach

Charleville

Vivier

Trier

Mézières

Sedan

Arlon

LUXEMBOURG

Meuse R.

Luxembourg City

Saar R.

FRANCE

Montmedy

Longwy

Esch

NINTH
XXXX
FIRST

Thionville

- - - ► PLANNED GERMAN ATTACKS

◄─── ACTUAL GERMAN ATTACKS

───── LIMIT OF GERMAN ADVANCE

Moselle R.

Metz

0   15 miles

0   15 km

5

Right:

There were many heroes during the fighting. Pvt. James R. Hendrix of the 53rd AIB, 4th Armd Div, at Assenois, on December 26, 1944, showed repeated heroism. His Medal of Honor citation said, "… *he was with the leading element engaged in the final thrust to break through to the besieged garrison at Bastogne when halted by a fierce combination of artillery and small arms fire. He dismounted from his halftrack and advanced against two 88mm guns, and, by the ferocity of his rifle fire, compelled the guncrews to take cover and then to surrender. Later in the attack he again left his vehicle, voluntarily, to aid two wounded soldiers, helpless and exposed to intense machinegun fire. Effectively silencing two hostile machineguns, he held off the enemy by his own fire until the wounded men were evacuated.*

"*Pvt. Hendrix again distinguished himself when he hastened to the aid of still another soldier who was trapped in a burning halftrack. Braving enemy sniper fire and exploding mines and ammunition in the vehicle, he extricated the wounded man and extinguished his flaming clothing, thereby saving the life of his fellow soldier …*" This memorial to Hendrix is at Assenois. http://www.travelsandtipples.com/

Below:

The disposition of the Allied forces at the start of the battle.

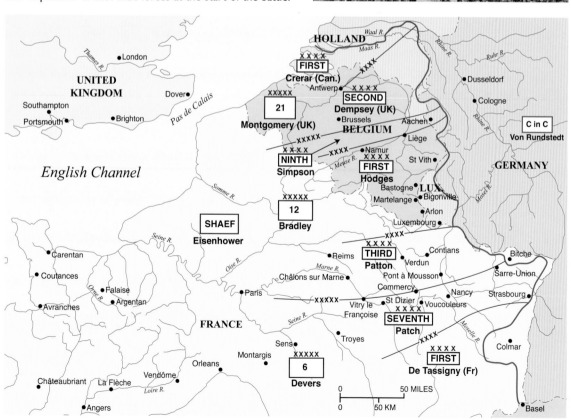

ORDER OF BATTLE OF THE FORCES IN BASTOGNE

Under the command of acting 101st Division commander: Brig-Gen. Anthony C. McAuliffe

Asst CO: Brig-Gen. Gerald J. Higgins

101st Airborne Division

501st Parachute Infantry Regiment (Lt-Col. Julian J. Ewell)

502nd Parachute Infantry Regiment (Lt-Col. Steve A. Chappuis)

506th Parachute Infantry Regiment (Col. Robert F. Sink)

327th Glider Infantry Regiment (Col. Joseph H. Harper)

321st Glider Field Artillery Battalion (Lt-Col. Edward L. Carmichael)

907th Glider Field Artillery Battalion (Lt-Col. Clarence F. Nelson)

377th Parachute Field Artillery Battalion (Lt-Col. Harry W. Elkins)

463rd Parachute Field Artillery Battalion (Lt-Col. John T. Cooper, Jr.)

81st Airborne Antiaircraft Battalion (Lt-Col. X. B. Cox, Jr.)

326th Airborne Engineer Battalion (Lt-Col. Hugh A. Mozley)

Combat Command B, 10th Armored Division
(Col. William L. Roberts)

3rd Tank Battalion (Lt-Col. Henry T. Cherry)

20th Armored Infantry Battalion (Maj. William R. Desobry)

54th Armored Infantry Battalion (Lt-Col. James O'Hara)

420th Armored Field Artillery Battalion (Lt-Col. Barry D. Browne)

705th Tank Destroyer Battalion (Lt-Col. Clifford D. Templeton)

755th Field Artillery Battalion

969th Field Artillery Battalion

Other troops

35th and 158th Combat Engineer Battalions; 58th and 420th Armored Field Artillery Battalions

Team SNAFU (mainly stragglers from 28th Inf Div)

Total: 22,800+ men

Battle Casualties

The Battle of the Bulge lasted for a full month, as measured from the start of the German offensive on the morning of December 16, 1944, to the moment when elements of First Army and Third Army joined hands at the village of Houffalize on January 16, 1945. Even then the fighting continued as the Germans withdrew, St. Vith only being retaken on the 23rd. By the end the battle had involved some 600,000 American troops, supported by British along the Meuse, and 400,000 Germans.

Casualties are often stated as approximately 80,000 on the Allied side and 100,000 Germans; however immediate post-battle reports or estimates are not necessarily accurate. A further study from the U.S. Dept. of the Army assessed 108,347 losses on the American side (19,246 dead, 62,489 wounded, 26,612 captured/missing), while the German High Command noted 81,834 total losses for the period December 16–January 26 on the entire Western front.

Assigning losses to any one stage of the battle is even more difficult, although in its 10-day defense of Bastogne, prior to relief by Third Army, the 101st Airborne Division is recorded as having lost 2,048 officers and men. Some 500 more were lost in the weeks that followed as the Screaming Eagles helped to defend Patton's corridor and push the Germans back from Bastogne.

Right:
Rendezvous with Destiny identifies the 101st's casualties from December 19 to January 6 as 341 killed, 1,691 wounded, and 516 missing. They included Capt. Preston E. Towns, OC C/327th GIR whose grave is at the U.S. cemetery, Hamm. The 10th Armored Division's CCB incurred c. 500 casualties.

Above:

The German offensive took place during the worst European winter in 50 years. "Weather is a weapon the German army used with success, especially in the Ardennes offensive," said von Rundstedt, the German *Oberbefehlshaber* West (Commander-in-Chief West), following his capture five months later.

Left and below left:

The German forces achieved almost complete surprise but none of the divisions attacking Bastogne was at full strength. Panzer Lehr had only 40% of its tanks, 60% of its guns, and 60% of its authorized strength; the 26th VG Div lacked a regiment; 2nd Pz Div was at 80% strength, but one of its regiments of grenadiers was on bicycles and was used only for replacements. Units that later reinforced XLVII Pz Korps ranged in strength from 50 to 70%.

Above right:

Civilians had a hard time of it. Two elderly refugees pass a knocked-out halftrack on the road to Bastogne.

Right:

The conditions for the infantry were extremely hard as is shown by this photo of T/Sgt. Gettings of the 320th Inf Regt, 35th Division (attached to Third Army). He's heating a can of rations during a quiet period southeast of Bastogne, January 7, 1945.

Left:

The face of battle. Sgt. Joseph Holmes of Co C, 320th Inf Regt, 35th Division, Third Army seen on January 10. Life at the sharp end was unremitting tough with a very low life expectancy. The USAREUR Battlebook says, "By the fall of 1944, the Army had grown to a strength of almost eight million soldiers ... [but it] had a serious personnel problem. The 81 rifle squads of a typical infantry division numbered a total of only 3,240 riflemen. The remainder of the 14,000 soldiers of the division performed other tasks. Some, including the artillery, armor, tank destroyer units, and others, were of the combat arms. The remainder handled the essential supply and administrative tasks to keep the division in action. The situation in the division repeated itself at higher echelons. At the field army level (roughly 350,000 men), about one soldier in seven was in the front line. In the European theater as a whole, Omar Bradley estimated that only one soldier out of fifteen fought with a rifle. Although riflemen were the minority in the Army, they suffered the highest casualty rate—83% in Normandy. Bradley later reported that three out of every four casualties came from a rifle platoon, and that the rate of loss in rifle platoons was 90%. Thus there began in Normandy and continued through December of 1944 a severe infantry shortage in Europe, compounded by Army decisions to send more riflemen to the Pacific. As the Battle of the Bulge started, Bradley was working hard to solve the problem, and found that the only way was to assign men from other skills—including AA artillerymen—to the infantry."

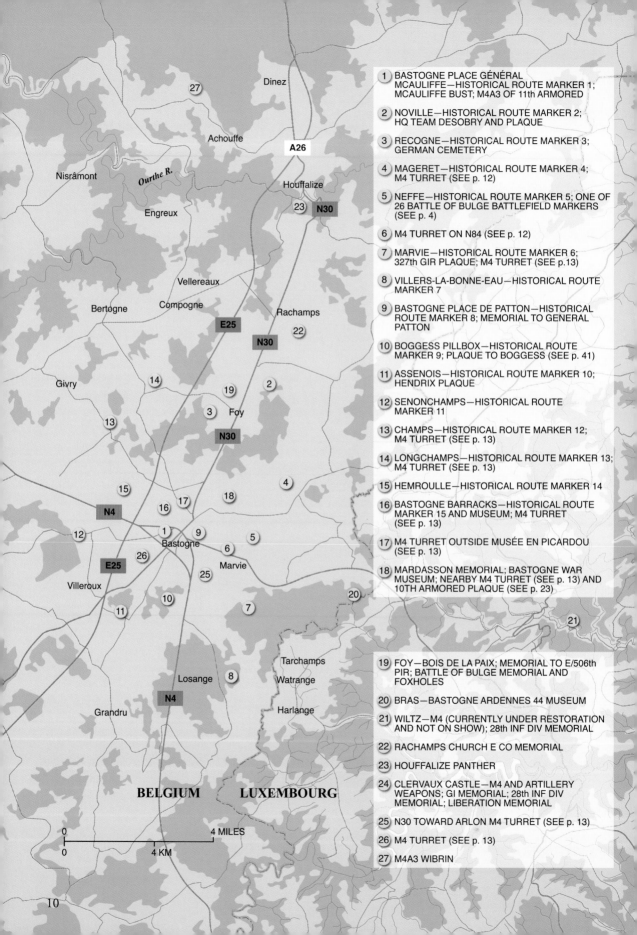

1 BASTOGNE PLACE GÉNÉRAL MCAULIFFE—HISTORICAL ROUTE MARKER 1; MCAULIFFE BUST; M4A3 OF 11th ARMORED

2 NOVILLE—HISTORICAL ROUTE MARKER 2; HQ TEAM DESOBRY AND PLAQUE

3 RECOGNE—HISTORICAL ROUTE MARKER 3; GERMAN CEMETERY

4 MAGERET—HISTORICAL ROUTE MARKER 4; M4 TURRET (SEE p. 12)

5 NEFFE—HISTORICAL ROUTE MARKER 5; ONE OF 26 BATTLE OF BULGE BATTLEFIELD MARKERS (SEE p. 4)

6 M4 TURRET ON N84 (SEE p. 12)

7 MARVIE—HISTORICAL ROUTE MARKER 6; 327th GIR PLAQUE; M4 TURRET (SEE p.13)

8 VILLERS-LA-BONNE-EAU—HISTORICAL ROUTE MARKER 7

9 BASTOGNE PLACE DE PATTON—HISTORICAL ROUTE MARKER 8; MEMORIAL TO GENERAL PATTON

10 BOGGESS PILLBOX—HISTORICAL ROUTE MARKER 9; PLAQUE TO BOGGESS (SEE p. 41)

11 ASSENOIS—HISTORICAL ROUTE MARKER 10; HENDRIX PLAQUE

12 SENONCHAMPS—HISTORICAL ROUTE MARKER 11

13 CHAMPS—HISTORICAL ROUTE MARKER 12; M4 TURRET (SEE p. 13)

14 LONGCHAMPS—HISTORICAL ROUTE MARKER 13; M4 TURRET (SEE p. 13)

15 HEMROULLE—HISTORICAL ROUTE MARKER 14

16 BASTOGNE BARRACKS—HISTORICAL ROUTE MARKER 15 AND MUSEUM; M4 TURRET (SEE p. 13)

17 M4 TURRET OUTSIDE MUSÉE EN PICARDOU (SEE p. 13)

18 MARDASSON MEMORIAL; BASTOGNE WAR MUSEUM; NEARBY M4 TURRET (SEE p. 13) AND 10TH ARMORED PLAQUE (SEE p. 23)

19 FOY—BOIS DE LA PAIX; MEMORIAL TO E/506th PIR; BATTLE OF BULGE MEMORIAL AND FOXHOLES

20 BRAS—BASTOGNE ARDENNES 44 MUSEUM

21 WILTZ—M4 (CURRENTLY UNDER RESTORATION AND NOT ON SHOW); 28th INF DIV MEMORIAL

22 RACHAMPS CHURCH E CO MEMORIAL

23 HOUFFALIZE PANTHER

24 CLERVAUX CASTLE—M4 AND ARTILLERY WEAPONS; GI MEMORIAL; 28th INF DIV MEMORIAL; LIBERATION MEMORIAL

25 N30 TOWARD ARLON M4 TURRET (SEE p. 13)

26 M4 TURRET (SEE p. 13)

27 M4A3 WIBRIN

Opposite:
Interesting locations around Bastogne today.

Left:
Clervaux boasts the CEBA (Study Group on the Battle of the Bulge) Memorial to the American infantryman.

Above:
Opposite Clervaux's GI memorial is this plaque remembering the liberation.

Below:
Taylor meets Middleton, VIII Corps commander, January 18. Taylor was handed a receipt: "Received from the 101st Airborne Division the town of Bastogne ... condition used but serviceable, Kraut disinfected."

1 There are a number of tank turrets on pedestals around Bastogne. These have moved over the years as is well covered by the STIWOT/Traces of War website. This T23 76mm-gun turret has 10th Armored markings and can be found on the N874 on the way to the Mardasson Memorial (18 on map on previous page).

2 This T23 turret has a 76mm gun and 10th Armored markings. It's on the N85 Rue de Neufchâteau before it passes under the N4 (26 on map). *Les Meloures/WikiCommons (CC BY-SA 3.0)*

3 This turret from an M4 (75mm) is on the N84 in the direction of Wiltz (6 on map). *Les Meloures/ WikiCommons (CC BY-SA 3.0)*

4 M4 (76mm) tank turret in Mageret, on the N874 Rue de Clervaux. The STIWOT analysis says it has moved from its original position on the N30 towards Houffalize. (4 on map).
Jeroen C. Koppes/TracesOfWar.com

5 Another M4 (76mm) turret, this one is on the N30 Rue de la Chappelle heading towards Arlon (25 on map).
Les Meloures/WikiCommons (CC BY-SA 3.0)

6 A turret with a difference: this one is from a Sherman Firefly equipped with a 17pdr gun. It can be found alongside the Musée en Piconrue, Place Saint-Pierre (17 on map). There's a text on its bustle: "37 Tank Batallion, 4th Armored Division, 1944–2004, Captain W. Dwight". *Jeroen C. Koppes/TracesOfWar.com*

7 On the N834 Rue de la Roche heading to Bertogne, just past Bastogne Barracks, is this M4 (75mm) turret (18 on map).
Agrillo Mario/WikiCommons (CC BY-SA 4.0)

8 Champs, on the N854, boasts this M4 (76mm). This is another of the turrets that has moved from its original position—on the road to Marche (13 on map).
Jeroen C. Koppes/TracesOf War.com

9 M34A1 turret from an M4 (75mm) in Marvie, off the N84, along the Rue de la Californie, alongside the sixth of Bastogne's Historical Route markers (7 on map).
Jeroen C. Koppes/TracesOf War.com

Opening Shots

Below right:
Destroyed during the Battle of Clervaux, after the war the burnt-out castle ruins were restored. Part now houses the Museum of the Battle of the Bulge. During the battle, a handful of 28th Infantry soldiers, led by Capt. John Aitken, were besieged by the German 2nd Panzer Division on December 17. The so-called Luxembourg Alamo. Outside are a number of guns and this M4A3 (76mm) of Co B, 2nd Tank Bn, U.S. 9th Armored Division, which supported the 28th Infantry.

Below:
America's most famous unit of WW2? In 2002 veterans of 101st's E Co, 506th PIR—the "Band of Brothers"—planted a tree as a memorial to their action at Rachamps.

AT 5:30 A.M. on December 16, some 500 concealed German artillery pieces suddenly opened up on the center of U.S. First Army's "quiet" sector. Beneath the 45-minute barrage hundreds of tank engines roared to life, even as Panzergrenadiers attacked or slipped in among U.S. outpost positions east of the Our in order to seize bridges over the river.

Two U.S. divisions lay directly in the path of Fifth Panzer Army's onslaught: the greenhorn 106th Infantry, which had arrived in its positions only a week earlier, and the bloodied 28th ID, which had just suffered over 5,000 casualties in the Huertgen Forest and had yet to receive sufficient replacements. The 106th would find two of its regiments cut off east of the Our, whereupon the mass surrender of nearly 8,000 troops would be the biggest American battlefield calamity since Bataan.

The 28th, "Bloody Bucket," Division put up a stand, however. The Germans were able to penetrate and peel off its 112th Regiment, to the north, and 109th Regiment, to the south, while its center 110th Regiment found itself isolated, taking the fullest brunt of the attack. The regiment fell back to the town of Clervaux, as Germans began pouring over the Our bridges. Then Clervaux itself was under assault, with the 28th's supporting tank battalion, the 707th, unable to cope with 2nd Panzer Division's spearheads. Neither could the 9th Armored Division's CCR, VIII Corps' only reserve, which found nearly every tank it sent up as reinforcement destroyed. The 110th Regiment's commander, Hurley Fuller, got on the radio, requesting permission to withdraw. While corps was instructing him to hold fast, a Panther pulled up and fired point blank into his headquarters.

The regiment broke up. Col. Fuller himself managed to escape with a few men, but was later captured in the woods. About 100 men continued to hold out in Clervaux's medieval castle, shooting down into passing enemy columns while they could. But the next day, out of ammo, and with a Mark IV breaking in through the gate, they surrendered. Some 350 men in the nearby village of Hosingen likewise succumbed. The 110th Regiment was veritably wiped out. 2nd Panzer, followed by the Panzer Lehr Division and 26th Volksgrenadier Division, headed onward toward Bastogne.

Left:
Men of the 110th Inf
Regt, 28th Inf Div in
Bastogne.

Below:
Hasso von Manteuffel's
German Fifth Panzer
Army's attack,
December 16–19. Held
up by valiant 28th
Infantry defense, the
timetable of the attack
was knocked out of
kilter. A number of
28th Infantry units
retreated to Bastogne
and played an
important part in the
defense.

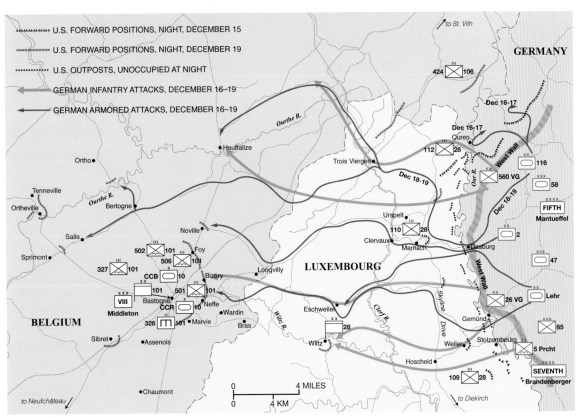

Right:

Wiltz in Luxembourg was the command post of Gen. Norman "Dutch" Cota's 28th Inf Div from December 19. The 28th played a valiant role in holding off the German attacks towards Bastogne. Hugh Cole sums it up:

"The fall of Wiltz ended the 28th Division's delaying action before Bastogne ... without the gallant bargain struck by the 110th Infantry and its Allied units—men for time—the German plans for a coup-de-main at Bastogne would have turned to accomplished fact."

Inset:

Memorial "To the 28th U.S. Infantry Division which liberated Wiltz on Sept 10th 1944 and gallantly defended our soil during the Battle of the Bulge."

Below:

The 155mm howitzers of the 969th FA Bn dug in, December 17. Artillery played an important role in the siege, particularly against armor. On December 20, for example, seven battalions fired 2,600 rounds solely at German armor.

Left:
Troops of the 28th Infantry Division, Bastogne, December 20. Some had lost their weapons during the German advance.

Below:
Elements of 110th Regiment, 28th Infantry Division who reached Bastogne at the beginning of the siege, regroup outside a garage on December 20. They would become part of Team Snafu along with stragglers from VIII Corps and elements of 9th Armored Division, under the command of 10th Armored's Col. Roberts.

This spread:
Then and now aerial views of Bastogne. **I** identifies the road running north and is visible at the lower left of the aerial recon photo. **2** identifies the main square, and **3** the course of the rue de Sablon.

As the massive offensive unfolded, reports reaching higher Allied HQ were unclear. Was this just a spoiling attack, designed to disrupt renewed U.S. thrusts toward the Saar and Ruhr? It was still hardly believed the Germans could mount a full-blooded strategic offensive at this point in the war.

Nevertheless, measures were taken. From the north, the 705th Tank Battalion was ordered to drive for Bastogne, having to dodge panzer spearheads en route. Various independent engineer and field artillery battalions were also ordered to the town, including the African-American 969th FA. From the south, Third Army's Patton was ordered to send his 10th Armored Division. He screamed mightily about it, since he had been about to launch his own offensive against the Saar, but did release the division's Combat Command B.

Orders also went out to the two U.S. airborne divisions—the 82nd and 101st—which had been resting near Reims, France. The 82nd had been pulled out of Holland first and was in better shape so it was on the road first, taking trucks past Bastogne to the embattled

town of St. Vith, farther north. Then the 101st was assembled. This was easier said than done since the Screaming Eagles had been out of the line for less than a month, had turned over most of their weapons, and officer teams had to scour Paris to fetch in men on leave. By the 18th enough vehicles (mainly open-air cattle trucks) had been assembled and the division took to the road, many of the paratroopers without guns or ammo.

When 10th Armored's CCB arrived in Bastogne its commander, Col. Roberts, was disgruntled at being ordered to split up his command. But the town of some 4,000 was the area's main road hub—thus an enemy magnet, not unlike Gettysburg in the Civil War—while it could not be clear from which direction the Germans would approach. While most of the Ardennes was rolling forest, Bastogne was on a clear plateau, surrounded by little villages. Roberts broke his command into three task forces (Team Desobry pushed NE to Noville; Team Cherry E to Longvilly, and Team O'Hara SE to Marvie), to intercept any enemy that arrived.

20

Bastogne has a special place in the annals of American military history and embodies the pluck and bloody-mindedness of the GI. Thanks to the tenacity of U.S. units to the east, Bastogne was not completely encircled until December 21, by which time its defenders had been swelled by CCB of the 10th Armd Div and part of the SHAEF theater reserve in the form of the doughty 101st Airborne, although without its CO.

1–4 The main street in Bastogne, the rue de Sablon, runs from the Place Général McAuliffe to today's Musée en Piconrue—in 1944 the Bethlehem Convent was used as a hospital in the siege.

2 Watercolor by Olin Dows (1904–81) of the gate of the Monastery command post of the 501st PIR from an upper floor window. Dows was in Bastogne in December and recorded impressions of the siege.

3 Men of 10th Armored on the Grand Rue (rue de Sablon), seen today at **4**. *BoomBoomBeem/WikiCommons (CC BY-SA 3.0)*

5 and 6 Then and now photos of Place Général McAuliffe. The round building on the today image is the tourist center. Note the M4A3 Sherman by the intersection. Named *Barracuda*, it served in Co B, 41st Tank Bn, 11th Armored Division. It was knocked out near Renaumont, west of Bastogne, on December 30.

Into Battle

Below:
Soldiers from the 101st move north, December 19. Note 2.36-inch bazooka crew. These teams would prove their worth over the days ahead with many successes—such as John Ballard who accounted for one of the two tanks destroyed by paratroopers around Champs on Christmas morning. But the U.S. Army bazooka wasn't the best. Gen. James M. Gavin said the 82nd "did not get adequate antitank weapons until it began to capture the first German Panzerfausts. By fall '44 we had truckloads of them ... They were the best hand-carried antitank weapon of the war."

Opposite, above:
Disposition of CCB 10th Armored, midnight December 18.

Opposite, below:
1/506th PIR head out to Noville to support Team Desobry who were hard pressed by 2nd Panzer Division, December 19.

THE 2ND PANZER Division had been having matters all its own way since the start of the offensive, shooting up some 60 U.S. tanks around Clervaux at the cost of only four of its own, destroying a task force of 9th Armored's CCR, and breaking into the open, already about a third of the way to its objective, the Meuse. But late on the 18th it came up against new opposition at the village of Noville, just five miles from Bastogne. It was Task Force Desobry of 10th Armored's CCB, which had just arrived. Together with remnants of 9th Armored and survivors of the 28th ID, the Tiger Division tankers were able to beat back the initial assault.

A key to the German offensive was that it was launched in dismal weather, which kept Allied air forces out of the battle. But that same factor wreaked havoc on the roads, causing gigantic traffic jams that slowed German infantry and artillery support. One more day and Bastogne would be easy picking for the Germans. However, during the dark, early morning hours of December 19 the 101st Airborne arrived at the town.

The paratroopers' advance toward forward positions was impeded by a veritable flood of retreating, often panicked, U.S. troops heading the other way, though this allowed the troopers to cadge weapons and ammo on their march. Under a morning fog the Germans attacked Noville again, as Panzergrenadiers slipped around it on both sides. The 10th Armored's TF Desobry lost half its vehicles and Desobry himself was seriously wounded, then captured when more penetrating Germans overran his medical aid station. The paratroopers fell back to Foy. At nearby Longville, the 10th CCB's Task Force Cherry, along with the HQ of the 9th's CCR, was overrun.

On the 21st the Panzer Lehr Division circuited Bastogne from the south, cutting off its contact with the rest of the U.S. front, while the 26th Volksgrenadier Division filled in the ring. The next day the Germans sent in an offer for the surrounded Americans to surrender. The temporary commander of the 101st Airborne, Anthony McAuliffe, replied with only one word: "Nuts." To him, the battle was just getting started.

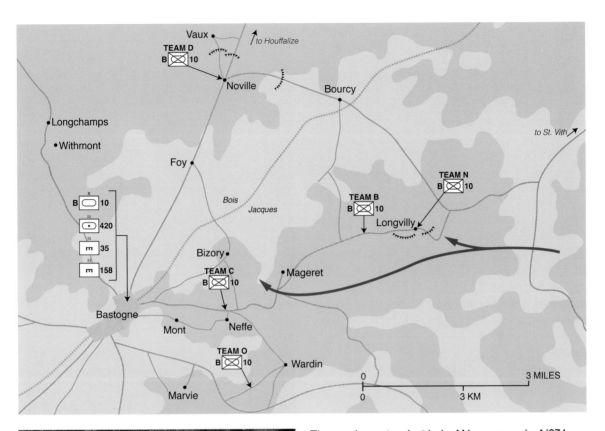

Vaux

↗ to Houffalize

TEAM D
B ⊠ 10

Noville

Bourcy

Longchamps

Withmont

↗ to St. Vith

Foy

TEAM N
B ⊠ 10

Bois
Jacques

TEAM B
B ⊠ 10

B ▭ 10

⊙ 420

Longvilly

m 35

m 158

Bizory

Mageret

TEAM C
B ⊠ 10

Bastogne

Mont

Neffe

TEAM O
B ⊠ 10

Wardin

Marvie

0   3 MILES

0   3 KM

The panel associated with the M4 turret on the N874 near the Mardasson Memorial (16 on map on p.10) reads: "*The US 10th Armored Division's Combat Command B, the first major combat unit to defend Bastogne, arrived on the evening of December 18, 1944. Col William L. Roberts deployed his Combat Command in three teams: Team Desobry at Noville, Team Cherry at Neffe and Longvilly, Team O'Hara at Wardin and Marvie. After delaying the initial German advance, the remnants of these 10th Armored teams joined the 101st Airborne Division for the remainder of the siege. In recognition of their gallant actions, Combat Command B was awarded the Presidential Unit Citation.*"

Above:
Another view of 1st Bn, 506th PIR heading out to Noville to support Team Desobry.

Below:
Elin Dows' sketch of the monastery used by 501st PIR as a command post.

Opposite, top:
The situation on December 19 shows the defense perimeter constructed and enemy attacks on Noville, Longvilly, and Neffe—usually small German combined arms forces, both with and without artillery support, infiltrating under cover of bad weather with the support (as shown in Olin Dows' painting on p.29), of tanks.

Opposite, below left:
Noville from the air.

Opposite, below right:
The CP of Major Desobry (commanding 10th Armored's Team Desobry) and Lt-Col. LaPrade (1st Bn 506th PIR). Team Desobry was sent to Noville and fought a delaying action allowing the defense perimeter to be set up. Eventually, an 88mm round exploded in the house, killing LaPrade and wounding Desobry who was taken prisoner by the Germans when the field hospital was captured. *Serjos de Groot/TracesOfWar.com*

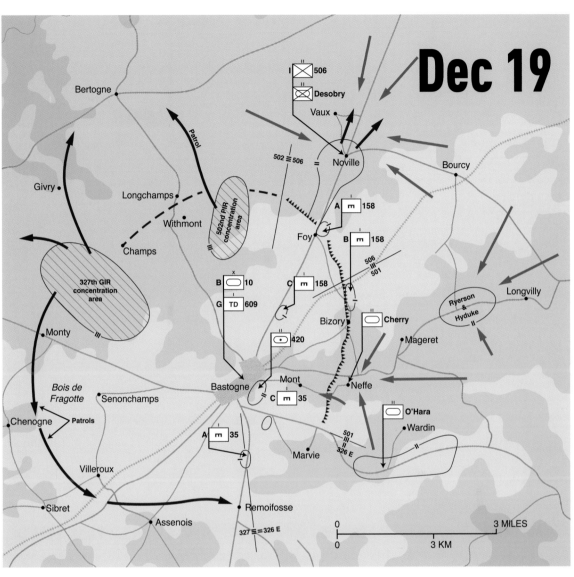

Dec 19

I ⊠ 506
⊠ **Desobry**

502 ≡ 506 =

Bertogne

Vaux •

Noville

Bourcy •

Givry •

Patrol

Longchamps •

Withmont •

502nd PIR concentration area

A m 158

Foy •

B m 158

Champs •

327th GIR concentration area

B 10

G TD 609

C m 158

506 / 501

Bizory •

Cherry

Mageret •

Ryerson & Hyduke

Longvilly •

Monty •

420

Bois de Fragotte

Senonchamps •

Mont •

C m 35

Neffe •

O'Hara

Wardin •

Chenogne •

Patrols

A m 35

Villeroux •

Marvie •

501 / 326 E

Sibret •

Remoifosse •

Assenois •

327 ≡≡ 326 E

0   3 MILES
0   3 KM

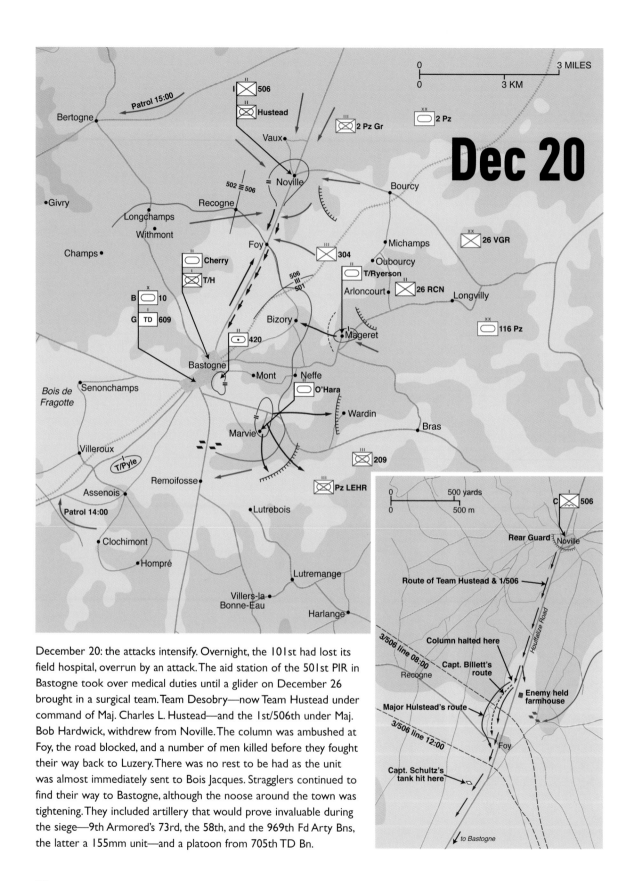

December 20: the attacks intensify. Overnight, the 101st had lost its field hospital, overrun by an attack. The aid station of the 501st PIR in Bastogne took over medical duties until a glider on December 26 brought in a surgical team. Team Desobry—now Team Hustead under command of Maj. Charles L. Hustead—and the 1st/506th under Maj. Bob Hardwick, withdrew from Noville. The column was ambushed at Foy, the road blocked, and a number of men killed before they fought their way back to Luzery. There was no rest to be had as the unit was almost immediately sent to Bois Jacques. Stragglers continued to find their way to Bastogne, although the noose around the town was tightening. They included artillery that would prove invaluable during the siege—9th Armored's 73rd, the 58th, and the 969th Fd Arty Bns, the latter a 155mm unit—and a platoon from 705th TD Bn.

Bois Jacques—Jack's Wood—manned by the Band of Brothers. The plaque on the monument (right) reads: "*May the world never forget. In the wood behind this monument, on 18 December 1944 'E' Company of the 506th PIR 101st Airborne Division dug their foxholes in the Bois Jacques Woods as part of the defense perimeter of Bastogne ... The circumstances were dreadful with constant mortar, rocket and artillery fire, snow fall, temperatures below -28 Celsius at night with little food and ammunition.... On December 24th the 'E' Company position was attacked at dawn by about 45 enemy soldiers. The attack failed and 'E' Company held their position with 1 casualty against 23 of the enemy. The position of 'E' Company was twice bombed and strafed by American P-47s. During the periods of January 9th and January 13th 'E' Company suffered its most casualties ending with the attack and capture of Foy on January 13th. 8 were killed in Foy and 6 earlier. During the whole period 32 were wounded and 21 were evacuated with cold weather illnesses ... This monument is dedicated to all that fought and is symbolic of what happened to other units during the Battle of the Bulge. Airborne Always*"
(Reenactor photo www.jeffpardoen.com.)

Above:
An atmospheric reenactor photograph of the 2005 Bastogne Historic Walk in realistic weather conditions. *www.jeffpardoen.com*

Below:
German PoWs dig graves for those killed defending Bastogne. Photo taken December 21.

Opposite, above:
With pressure from command to push beyond Bastogne, German Fifth Panzer Army and XLVII Corps decided that Panzer Lehr should take Bastogne while the other forces continued west. A key element in the defense of Bastogne in this period was the artillery. Col. Ralph M. Mitchell in his CSI publication on the defense of Bastogne discusses the success of the guns during the period, citing high morale, good positioning, and excellent training. On December 20 alone, he notes, seven battalions fired 2,600 rounds solely at enemy armor. "Firing in the direct and indirect mode, artillery was effective against German tanks ... no German tank within range of American artillery was safe." Isolated vehicles that penetrated the defensive lines were polished off by bazooka teams.

Opposite, below:
The outskirts of Neffe by war artist Olin Dows. Dows spent a year in England before D-Day and then traveled to Normandy as part of the 166th Signal Unit. He was assigned to Bastogne in late December, and witnessed the siege of the city. This shows German forces preparing to attack 3rd/501st on the night of December 20. They were seen off by a combination of the infantry and 1st Pl B/705th TD Bn which destroyed three SP guns and whose MGs helped kill numerous of the enemy caught between the barbed wire fences visible in the painting.

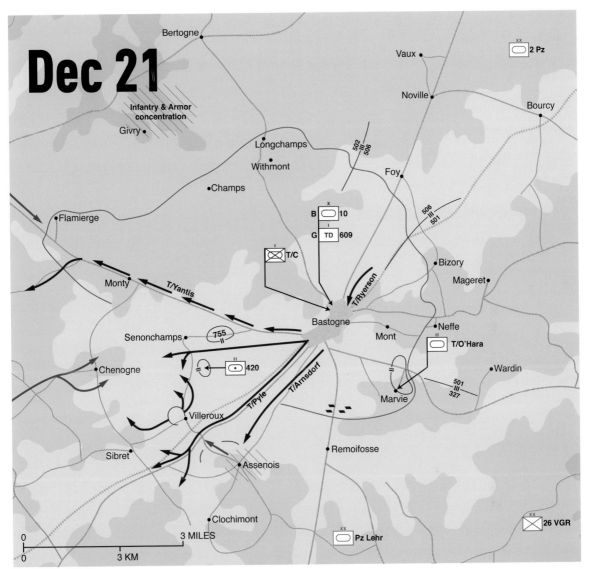

Dec 21

Bertogne

Vaux

Noville

Bourcy

XX ☐ **2 Pz**

Infantry & Armor
concentration

Givry

Longchamps

Withmont

Foy

502
III
506

Champs

Flamierge

B ☐ **10**

G ☐ TD **609**

506
III
501

Bizory

Mageret

⊠ **T/C**

T/Ryerson

Monty

T/Yantis

Bastogne

Neffe

Mont

☐ **T/O'Hara**

Senonchamps

〔 **755** 〕
‖

Wardin

Chenogne

‖ ⊡ **420**

T/Pyle

T/Arnsdorf

Villeroux

‖

Marvie

501
III
327

Sibret

Assenois

Remoifosse

Clochimont

0 _____ 3 MILES

0 _____ 3 KM

XX ☐ **Pz Lehr**

XX ⊠ **26 VGR**

Dows '45.

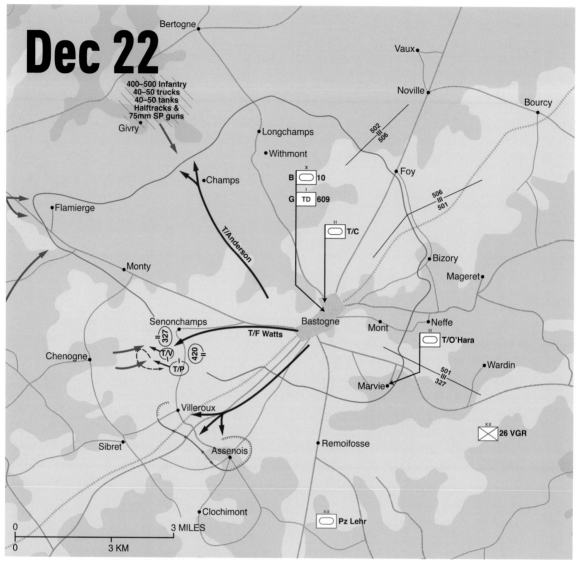

Dec 22

400–500 Infantry
40–50 trucks
40–50 tanks
Halftracks &
75mm SP guns

Bertogne

Vaux

Noville

Bourcy

Givry

Longchamps

502 / III / 506

Foy

Withmont

B ☰ 10

G | TD | 609

T/C

Champs

Flamierge

506 / III / 501

T/Anderson

Bizory

Mageret

Monty

Senonchamps

☰ 327

Bastogne

Mont

Neffe

T/O'Hara

T/F Watts

T/N

420 ☰

Chenogne

T/P

501 / III / 327

Wardin

Marvie

Villeroux

Sibret

Assenois

Remoifosse

26 VGR

Clochimont

Pz Lehr

0 ─────── 3 MILES
0 ─────── 3 KM

Above:

The envelopment of Bastogne was completed on the 21st, but as Mitchell says, "Though surrounded, the 101st was not cut off." Panzer Lehr didn't accomplish its mission on December 20th and tried again with 26th VG Division on the 21st. The perimeter tightened, but held, and on the night of the 21st Manteuffel and XVLII Korps commander, Heinrich Freiherr von Lüttwitz, decided to send a letter to the commander of the Bastogne garrison.

Left:

This painting of the 101st's message center by Olin Dows highlights another of the strengths of the defenders: the work of 101st Signal Co. Luckily, when they ran out of batteries on the 23rd, a new supply came in by air.

Nuts

At 11:30 On December 22, four Germans approached American lines south of Bastogne. The senior officer explained that they had a written message to be presented to the American commander of the town. They were taken first to the Kessler farmhouse and then to the F/327th GIR Command Post from where the message went to the Battalion Command Post in Marvie, then the 327th HQ and finally to Division HQ. Acting Chief of Staff, Lt-Col. Ned Moore entered Brig-Gen. Anthony C. McAuliffe's sleeping quarters and told him, "The Germans have sent some people forward to take our surrender." Moore recalled that McAuliffe, still half asleep, said "Nuts!" and started to climb out of his sleeping bag. The Division Operations Officer, Lt-Col. Harry Kinnard, remembered later that McAuliffe initially asked, "They want to surrender?" Moore told him, "No sir, they want us to surrender." McAuliffe erupted in anger, which shocked those looking on. He took the paper, looked at it, said, "Us surrender, aw nuts!" and dropped it on the floor. A little later he was informed that the German officers were still waiting for a formal reply at the F Company Command Post. McAuliffe wondered aloud, "Well, I don't know what to tell them." Kinnard said, "What you said initially would be hard to beat.... Sir, you said nuts." All members of the staff enthusiastically agreed, so McAuliffe said, "Have it typed up."

The 327th PIR commander, Col. Joseph W. Harper, took the reply back to the F Company Command Post and informed the senior German officer that he had the American Commander's reply. The German—who was blindfolded—asked if the reply was affirmative. Harper said, "The reply consists of a single word: Nuts! ... If you continue this foolish attack, your losses will be tremendous."

The two blindfolded German officers were then driven back to the Kessler farm. At the farm, the blindfolds were removed and the Germans opened the reply but didn't understand it. "What does this mean?"

"You can go to Hell," said Harper, who went on, "If you continue to attack, we will kill every goddamn German that tries to break into this city." The German replied, "We will kill many Americans. This is war." Harper then said, "On your way Bud, and good luck to you."

McAuliffe turned the incident to good advantage, providing his command with a Christmas message shown at right.

What's merry about all this, you ask? We're fighting – it's cold – we aren't home. All true, but what has the proud Eagle Division accomplished with its worthy comrades of the 10th Armored Division, the 705th Tank Destroyer Battalion and all the rest? Just this: We have stopped cold everything that has been thrown at us from the North, East, South, and West. We have identifications from four German Panzer Divisions, two German Infantry Divisions and one German Parachute Division. These units, spearheading the last desperate German lunge, were headed straight west for key points when the Eagle Division was hurriedly ordered to stem the advance. How effectively this was done will be written in history; not alone in our Division's glorious history but in world history. The Germans actually did surround us, their radios blared our doom. Their Commander demanded our surrender in the following impudent arrogance:

December 22d 1944

"To the U.S.A. Commander of the encircled town of Bastogne:

"The fortune of war is changing. This time the U.S.A. forces in and near Bastogne have been encircled by strong German armored units. More German armored units have crossed the river Ourthe near Ortheuville, have taken Marche and reached St. Hubert by passing through Hompre–Sibret–Tillet. Libramont is in German hands.

"There is only one possibility to save the encircled U.S.A. troops from total annihilation: that is the honorable surrender of the encircled town. In order to think it over a term of two hours will be granted beginning with the presentation of this note.

"If this proposal should be rejected one German Artillery Corps and six heavy A. A. Battalions are ready to annihilate the U.S.A. troops in and near Bastogne. The order for firing will be given immediately after this two hours' term.

"All the serious civilian losses caused by this artillery fire would not correspond with the well-known American humanity.

The German Commander"

The German Commander received the following reply:

22 December 1944

"To The German Commander:
N U T S!
The American Commander"

Allied Troops are counterattacking in force. We continue to hold Bastogne. By holding Bastogne we assure the success of the Allied Armies. We know that our Division Commander, General Taylor, will say: "Well Done!"

We are giving our country and our loved ones at home a worthy Christmas present and being privileged to take part in this gallant feat of arms are truly making for ourselves a Merry Christmas.

A. C. McAuliffe
Commanding

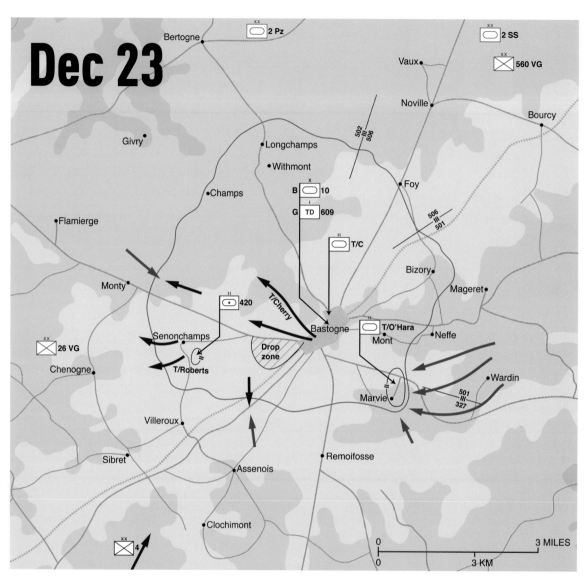

Dec 23

Bertogne	2 Pz	2 SS
		560 VG
Vaux		
Noville	Bourcy	

502 ─III─ 506

Givry

Longchamps

Withmont

Champs

Foy

B 10
G TD 609

506 ─III─ 501

Flamierge

T/C

Bizory

Mageret

Monty

420

T/Cherry

Bastogne

T/O'Hara

Neffe

26 VG

Senonchamps

Drop zone

Mont

Chenogne

T/Roberts

Wardin

Villeroux

Marvie

501 ─III─ 327

Sibret

Assenois

Remoifosse

Clochimont

4

0   3 MILES
0   3 KM

Gen George S. Patton
and Gen Anthony Mc Auliffe
just front of the Nuts Cave
Dec 30th, 1944

Opposite, above:
On the 23rd there were attacks to the west and southeast, but the weather had cleared and U.S. airpower was able to help negate them. Aerial resupply helped morale, and provided much needed medical supplies and ammunition.

Opposite, below:
These barracks were the site of the HQ of Gen. McAuliffe. His office has been preserved. *www.militarialagleize1944.com*

Above left:
The 705th TD Bn arrived in Bastogne late on the night of December 19, being attached to 101st Airborne the next day. Throughout the siege, the battalion destroyed around 40 German tanks and lost only six M18s. Supplemented by around 40 M4 mediums, the armor acted as a fire brigade, rushing to each hotspot.

Center left:
A bazooka position protects one of the roads into Bastogne, December 23.

Below left:
C-47A-40-DL 42-24051 of 73rd Troop Carrier Sqn, 434th Troop Carrier Gp, is dropping supplies to the Bastogne defenders. Poor weather and solid cloud cover over the town meant that Pathfinders had to drop to set up Eureka beacons for the C-47s to home in on. Each C-47 carried some 1,200lb of supplies, and on December 23 in just over four hours, 241 planes dropped 144 tons of supplies. Three days later there was a glider drop, ten carrying fuel and one a much-needed surgical team. Throughout the 26th, there were additional resupply sorties. The next day the last of the aerial resupply missions came in two waves. The first had few problems; the second, towing 50 gliders loaded with ammunition, had more difficulty, losing 13 aircraft and 17 gliders.

Above and below:
Another of Olin Dows' atmospheric paintings shows a Relief Station at Bastogne. The 326th Airborne Medical Co moved to the town by lorry from Mourmelon on December 16. There were some 17 ambulance-jeeps spread around the units to transport the wounded from the Battalion Aid Stations to the Division Clearing Station.
(*Bottom photo www.jeffpardoen.com.*)

Left:
A Luftwaffe bomb on December 24 landed on the 10th Armored field hospital on Rue de Neufchatel, near Place de McAuliffe. Amongst the 30 dead was nurse Renée LeMaire.

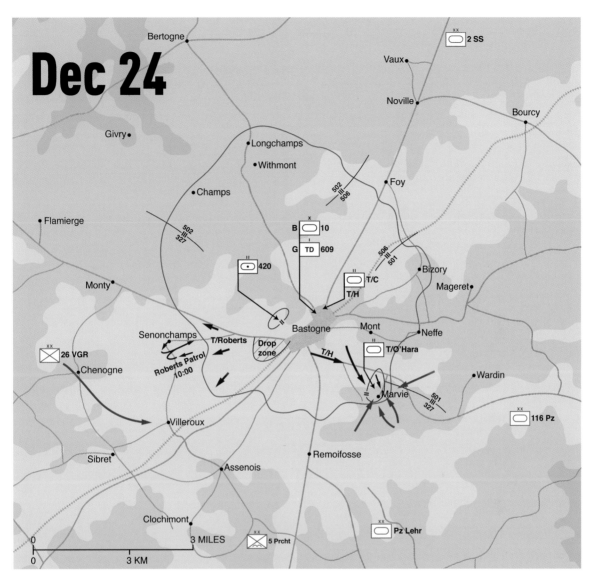

Dec 24

Bertogne

Vaux

XX
2 SS

Noville

Bourcy

Givry

Longchamps

•Withmont

Foy

502
III
506

•Champs

Flamierge

502
III
327

B 10
X

G TD 609
I

420

506
III
501

•Bizory

Mageret•

T/C
II

T/H

Monty

Bastogne

Mont

•Neffe

Senonchamps

T/Roberts Drop zone

T/O'Harra
II

26 VGR
XX

•Chenogne

Roberts Patrol
10:00

T/H

= •Marvie

•Wardin

501
III
327

116 Pz
XX

•Villeroux

Sibret

•Assenois

•Remoifosse

Clochimont

0 _____ 3 MILES
0 _____ 3 KM

5 Prcht
XX

Pz Lehr
XX

Above:
The German attackers were promised reinforcements but the attacks on December 24/25 were uncoordinated and failed. There is no doubt that the defenders were lucky that major attacks did not take place.

Left:
Enemy shells may scream overhead, but members of the 101st Airborne are still singing carols during a midnight Christmas service. Shortly after this photo was taken enemy bombers broke up the service.

Brig-Gen. Anthony McAuliffe (1898–1975)
Originally in charge of 101st Airborne's artillery when he dropped into Normandy, Gen. Don Pratt's death on D-Day saw him promoted to assistant divisional commander. As Maxwell Taylor (seen top left on January 5) was in the U.S. when the Battle of the Bulge started, it was McAuliffe who saved the day, and after whom the main square in Bastogne is named. His bust sits next to a 10th Armored M4 in the square, although the position has changed slightly since inauguration.
Battledetective.com

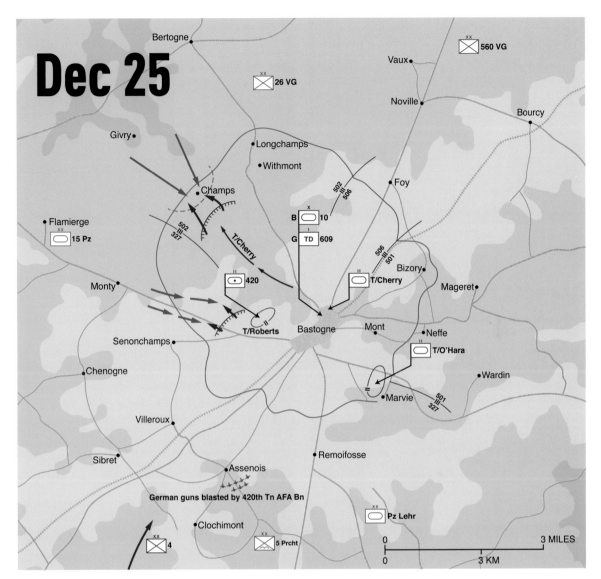

Dec 25

560 VG

Vaux

26 VG

Noville

Bourcy

Bertogne

Givry

Longchamps

Withmont

Foy

502
506

Champs

B | 10

Flamierge

502
327

G | TD | 609

15 Pz

T/Cherry

506
501

Bizory

420

T/Cherry

Mageret

Monty

T/Roberts

Bastogne

Mont

Neffe

Senonchamps

T/O'Hara

Chenogne

Wardin

Villeroux

Marvie

501
327

Sibret

Remoifosse

Assenois

German guns blasted by 420th Tn AFA Bn

Pz Lehr

Clochimont

4

5 Prcht

| 0 | | 3 MILES |
| 0 | | 3 KM |

By December 23, even as Panzer spearheads drove on for the Meuse, elements of nine German divisions surrounded Bastogne. Paratroopers of the 101st Division, manning lonely foxholes in woods and fields on the town's periphery, fought off German assaults by day and endured artillery barrages at night. Inside the town, ammunition was running short, artillery units had become rationed to ten rounds a day, and medical supplies had become critically scarce for the increasing hundreds of wounded.

But that day, a week into the offensive, the skies finally cleared and 2,000 Allied planes took to the air. Some 250 of these were cargo-bearing C-47s heading straight for Bastogne, their multicolored parachutes full of ammo, medicine and food, all a godsend to the beleaguered garrison. P-47s and Typhoons bombed and rocketed German frontline positions while heavies flew onward to plaster enemy supply routes.

Above:

As Third Army units reached Assenois, there were German thrusts towards Champs and Senonchamps.

Above left and right:
Officers of the 101st Airborne Division have Christmas dinner in Bastogne (Left; recreated Right) while the city is under German siege. Brig-Gen. Anthony McAuliffe is fourth on left.
Battledetective.com

Right:
Kampfgruppe Maucke attacked and broke through between the 327th GIR and 502nd PIR at Champs on Christmas morning. Hard fighting and help from 705th TD Bn saw them off as this KO'd PzKpfw IV attests.

Below left:
German dead after the Christmas Day fighting.

The 23rd also saw the expiration of Sixth SS Panzer Army's drive in the north as its spearhead, Kampfgruppe Peiper, abandoned its equipment and retreated. Hitler switched the entire focus of the offensive to the south, which meant that the bleeding sore of Bastogne had to be eliminated. It became a race to see who could get there first: Patton's reinforcing Third Army or a new flood of SS troops pouring down from the north.

Though on the 24th Patton wired McAuliffe that he should expect a good Christmas present, Third Army's armor had not yet shown up. Instead the Germans delivered their own present on Christmas Eve—over 100 Luftwaffe bombers, mainly Ju88s, plastering the center of the town. One bomb hit a medical aid station, killing over two dozen GI's, plus one of two gallant Belgian nurses who had assisted the wounded. The other, a native of the Congo, continued to care for the injured.

On Christmas morning German tanks roared up against the perimeter in the west; but the defenders had prepared interlocking fields of fire and knocked out 15 panzers while 101st paratroopers and glidermen doggedly held on to village strongpoints. It was an all-out effort, on Hitler's orders, to finally break the resistance at Bastogne; however, the weary, gallant defenders still refused to give in. Now that Allied airpower was in the battle, frontline German divisions were having their own problems with ammo stocks and fuel supply.

Below left:
Civilians trying to escape Bastogne are turned back by a 502nd PIR roadblock.

Below:
Olin Dows' "Winter Chow Line At Hemroulle."

Opposite, below right:
The plaque at Longchamps—"Near here, on the line Longchamps-Monaville in December 1944, the 2/502nd PIR supported by 101st Airborne's A/Tk/AA battalion defended the perimeter of Bastogne with courage." A nearby board tells the story— *"The village of Longchamps belonged to the same defense system as Champs, i.e. that is to say that it was allotted to the 502nd parachute regiment under the command of Lieutenant-Colonel Steve A. CHAPPUIS, with, in his line, the 506th Battalion, which defended the perimeter until Foy" and "For two days, the German forces tried to pierce the defenses set up by the 502nd regiment, who were well defended by an anti-aircraft regiment and despite sustaining serious casualties, held on. The survivors called this place 'misery wood'."* http://www.travelsandtipples.com/

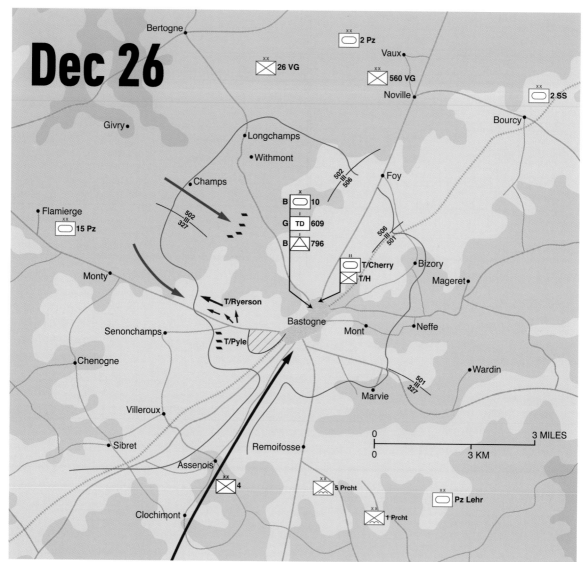

Dec 26

Bertogne

2 Pz
Vaux

26 VG

560 VG
Noville

2 SS
Bourcy

Givry

Longchamps

Withmont

Foy

Champs

502 III 506

B x 10

Flamierge

15 Pz

502 III 327

G I TD 609

B 796

506 III 501

Bizory

T/Cherry

T/H

Mageret

Monty

T/Ryerson

Bastogne

Mont

Neffe

Senonchamps

T/Pyle

Chenogne

Wardin

Marvie

501 III 327

Villeroux

0   3 MILES

Sibret

0   3 KM

Remoifosse

Assenois

4

5 Prcht

Pz Lehr

Clochimont

1 Prcht

Above:
The attacks at Champs and Mont were nowhere near as intensive as the previous day's. The main interest for the defenders was the airdrop of supplies and the arrival, that evening, of the lead tank of 4th Armored. The siege had been lifted!

Left:
101st infantrymen pass a signpost to Marvie as they head out of Bastogne to attack the Germans.

Opposite, center:
"Two Way Traffic at Bastogne," by Olin Dows.

Opposite, below:
Patton's *After Action Report* illustrates Third Army's attack.

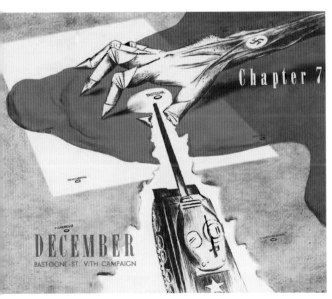

Chapter 7

DECEMBER
BASTOGNE-ST. VITH CAMPAIGN

Top left and right:

1-Lt. Charles Boggess, Cpl. Milton Dickerman and Pvts. James G. Murphy, Hubert S. Smith and Harold Hafner pose on their M4A3E2 Sherman Jumbo *Cobra King*. They had led the final dash into Bastogne and linked up with the A/326th AB Engr Bn of the 101st Airborne, at a pillbox about two miles from the town center. The plaque on this bunker reads: "*In memory of Lt Charles P. Boggess (1911–1985) whose tank was the first to break the encirclement of Bastogne. Here, in the evening of December 26, 1944, 4th Armored Division of Patton's Third Army met with 101st Airborne Division thus breaking the encirclement of Bastogne.*" In March 1945 *Cobra King* had its 75mm replaced by a 76mm main gun and ended up as a gate guardian for Rose Barracks in Vilseck, Germany. Restoration by the Patton Museum included replacing the original 75mm with one found on another vehicle.

Above:
December 26—the day the garrison was reached by 4th Armored—as 101st Airborne watched C-47s drop supplies. Resupply by air—particularly of ammunition—was difficult because of the weather but helped keep the garrison alive.

Left:
One of Kampfgruppe Maucke's PzKpfw IVs abandoned at Champs after the Christmas Day fighting. This one was named "The Happy Salamander." *BattleDetective.com*

Right:
Poor old Bastogne! Bloody but unbowed. Smoke rises from buildings smoldering after a Luftwaffe attack, as residents of the town flee in order to avoid bombing and shelling. The bustling modern town does not hide its wartime associations and is a center for military enthusiasts. Note then and now corner (A).

Patton to the Rescue

THOUGH AT FIRST Patton had only begrudgingly lent his 10th Armored's CCB to the defense of Bastogne, once he realized the offensive was a full-blooded German effort he reoriented his entire III Corps, led by the 4th Armored Division, to be followed by the XII Corps, to head north. His attack kicked off on December 22, but the roads were no better for his armor than they were for Manteuffel's, and in addition he met the 5th Fallschirmjäger Division of German Seventh Army along the way. The tough German paratroopers, who received timely Panzerjäger support, held up his lead columns time and again, forcing the spearhead 4th Armored to fight for every inch of its advance.

As Patton's troops got closer to Bastogne, the Germans surrounding it likewise turned to fend them off. On December 26, Lt. Colonel Creighton Abrams, leading 37th Battalion of 4th Armored's CCR, finally reached the perimeter, and paused to decide what to do. Bristling German strongpoints were on every side so there was no safe option.

But while he stood there Abrams witnessed another desperate airlift of supplies to Bastogne. He decided to simply go hell-bent for the town, and after running a gauntlet of fire, at 4:50 in the afternoon, five Shermans of Company B made it through. The arrival of Third Army tanks was met with jubilation by the defenders of Bastogne—the ring had been broken and they were restored to the U.S. front.

On that day, too, the 2nd Panzer Division, whose advance elements had come within sight of the Meuse, was hammered back from its objective by the U.S. 2nd Armored. During the following days the Germans would pound at Third Army's thin relief corridor to Bastogne, even as Patton's follow-up divisions sought to expand it. But by then the Germans had given up on the initial, grandiose goal of their offensive, and only sought to forestall further Allied offensives. Weeks of vicious attrition fighting would follow; however, Patton's arrival at Bastogne had sealed the fate of Hitler's last great gamble in the West.

Below:
Patton's memorial in Bastogne is the focus of regular events to commemorate the anniversary of the battle.
U.S. Navy/Mate 1st Class Ted Banks/ WikiCommons

Below right:
Eisenhower, Bradley, and Patton met at Verdun on December 19. It was Patton's finest hour. He promised that Third Army would attack immediately.

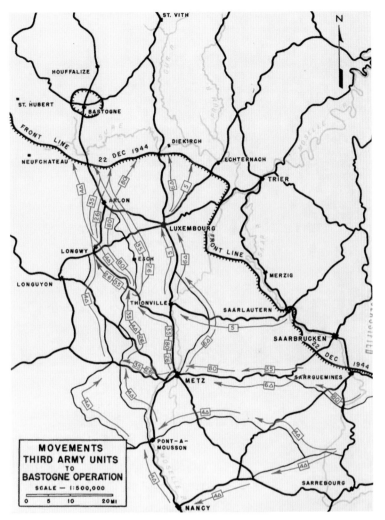

MOVEMENTS
THIRD ARMY UNITS
TO
BASTOGNE OPERATION
SCALE — 1:500,000
0   5   10   20 MI

Left:

Alerted to the Ardennes offensive by his brilliant Intelligence Officer, Brig-Gen. Oscar Koch, Patton had asked his staff to prepare to attack north from their current positions on the Saar. Reaching their start line on December 22, they reached Bastogne four days later after very hard fighting. This map from Patton's *After Action Report* shows the initial stages of their journey.

Above:

Stele in Arlon: "From this point on December 24, 1944, Gen Patton sent forth Third Army into the Battle of the Ardennes."

Left:

Patton's Third Army was blessed with two crack armored divisions, the 4th and 6th. The former included the 37th Tank Bn commanded by Lt-Col. Creighton Abrams, who would go on to become Chief of Staff of the U.S. Army and have the current U.S. MBT named in his honor. This is Blockbuster 3d, the command tank of B/37th Tank Bn, Capt. James Leach's vehicle. Leach and John Whitehall, OC A/37, both won DSCs on the road to Bastogne.

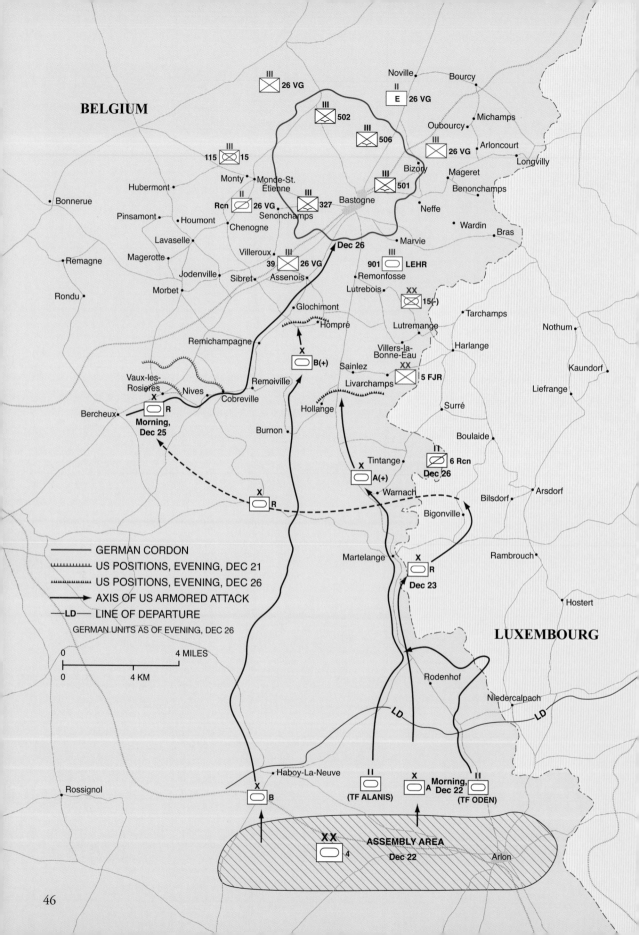

BELGIUM

III
26 VG

II
E 26 VG

Noville

Bourcy

III
502

Oubourcy

Michamps

III
506

III
26 VG

Arloncourt

115 III 15

Monty
Monde-St.
Étienne

Bizory

Longvilly

Hubermont

III
501

Mageret

Bonnerue

Pinsamont

Houmont

II
Rcn 26 VG

Benonchamps

Bastogne

III
327

Lavaselle

Chenogne

Senonchamps

Neffe

Bras

Remagne

Magerotte

Villeroux

III
39 26 VG

Dec 26

Marvie

Wardin

Rondu

Jodenville

Sibret

Assenois

III
901 LEHR

Remonfosse

Morbet

Glochimont

Hompré

Lutrebois

XX
15(-)

Tarchamps

Nothum

Remichampagne

Lutremange

Harlange

Kaundorf

Vaux-les-
Rosières

Nives

Cobreville

Remoiville

X
B(+)

Villers-la-
Bonne-Eau

XX
5 FJR

Liefrange

Sainlez

Livarchamps

Bercheux

X R

Morning,
Dec 25

Burnon

Hollange

Surré

Boulaide

Arsdorf

Tintange

II
6 Rcn
Dec 26

X
A(+)

Warnach

Bilsdorf

X R

Bigonville

Rambrouch

GERMAN CORDON

Martelange

X R

Hostert

US POSITIONS, EVENING, DEC 21

US POSITIONS, EVENING, DEC 26

Dec 23

AXIS OF US ARMORED ATTACK

LUXEMBOURG

LD LINE OF DEPARTURE

GERMAN UNITS AS OF EVENING, DEC 26

Rodenhof

0   4 MILES

Niedercalpach

0   4 KM

LD

LD

Haboy-La-Neuve

X B

Rossignol

Morning,
Dec 22

II
(TF ALANIS)

X A

II
(TF ODEN)

XX
4

ASSEMBLY AREA

Dec 22

Arlon

46

Opposite:
From their concentration area 4th Armored attacked northward creating a corridor through to Bastogne.

Left:
A 25th Cav jeep destroyed during the fighting on the road to Chaumont on December 27th.

Below:
The gunner on a 4th Armored halftrack loads a new belt of .50cal.

Bottom:
Lt-Gen. George Patton (right), Lt-Col. Steve A. Chappuis (center, commanding 2/502nd PIR), and Brig-Gen. Anthony McAuliffe on the steps of Chateau de Rolley after Patton had given them the DSC. Today the building behind them has been remodeled.
Battledetective.com

Elements of Third Army punched through to Bastogne from the southwest. They met the 326th Engineers at around 16:50 on December 26. A day later Gen. Maxwell D. Taylor reached Bastogne with the 4th Armored and resumed command of the 101st Airborne. The battle didn't stop there: immediately after the siege had been lifted, Third Army fought to widen the narrow corridor to Bastogne before moving on northward to crush the remnants of the attacking force.

Above:
Infantrymen of the 10th AIB, 4th Armored, cross snowy fields in open order towards Bastogne on December 27.

Below:
A classic view of 4th Armored in the snow around Bastogne, showing men from an AIB passing a White halftrack.

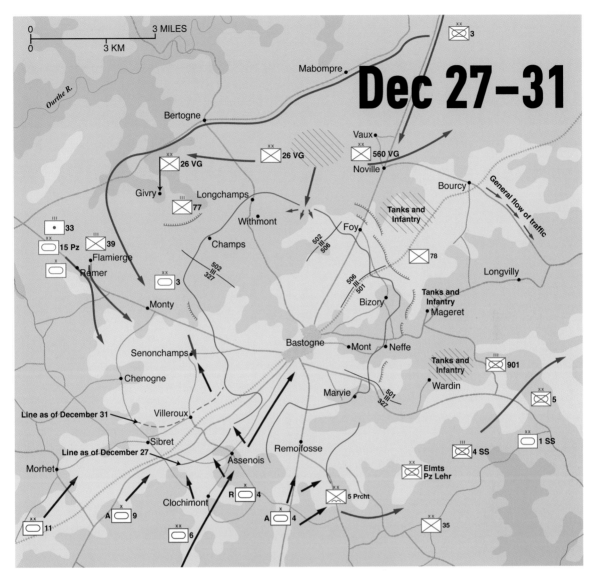

Dec 27–31

0 — 3 MILES
0 — 3 KM

Ourthe R.

Mabompre

3 (XX)

Bertogne

Vaux
26 VG (XX)
560 VG (XX)
Noville

26 VG (XX)
Givry
Longchamps
77 (III)
Withmont
Foy
502 / III / 506
Bourcy

General flow of traffic

Tanks and Infantry

33 (III)
15 Pz (XX)
39 (III)
Champs
Remer
3 (XX)
502 / III / 327
Monty
506 / III / 501
Bizory
78 (XX)
Longvilly

Flamierge

Tanks and Infantry
Mageret

Senonchamps
Bastogne
Mont
Neffe
Tanks and Infantry
Wardin
901 (III)

Chenogne
5 (XX)
Villeroux
Marvie
501 / III / 327
1 SS (XX)

Line as of December 31
Sibret
Remoifosse
4 SS (III)

Line as of December 27
Assenois
Elmts Pz Lehr (XX)
Morhet
R 4 (X)
5 Prcht (XX)
35 (XX)

Clochimont
A 9 (X)
A 4 (X)
11 (XX)
6 (XX)

Above:
This map highlights the breaking of the siege and consolidation of the position. *Rendezvous with Destiny* quotes Patton: "Unquestionably this was the critical day of the operation [the 30th] as there was a concerted effort on the part of the Germans, using at least five divisions, to again isolate Bastogne."

Left:
Private Frank Kelly, an MP from 4th Armored, leads prisoners to the rear.

Opposite, above:
Following a night skirmish near Bastogne on December 30, members of the 101st Airborne Division set out to find and rejoin their unit.

Opposite, below:
Reenactment photo from a Bastogne Historical Walk. *www.jeffpardoen.com*

Above left:
One result of bombing on the night of December 29–30 was the destruction of the command post of CCB, 10th Armored. Here, the next day, anxious men hope to find some signs of life among the wreckage.

Left:
Once the siege had been broken, refugees began to leave Bastogne. This is in the main square now named after Brig-Gen. Anthony McAuliffe.

Below:
The same scene today, the view blocked by Bastogne's Tourist Information Center also prominent in the aerial view of the square (see p. 20).

Right:
Track change for a 6th Armored M4—not much fun in freezing conditions.

Below right:
The 4th Armored M18 Hellcat TD in the foreground was knocked out by German artillery fire near Sibret, December 29.

Bottom right:
This is all that remains of trucks carrying fuel to the troops at Bastogne after an ambush on January 2.

Opposite, top:
Men of the 101st Airborne move out of Bastogne on December 29.

Opposite, center left:
Gen. Patton's *After Action Report*—January, End of the Bulge.

Opposite, center right:
Memorial honoring the 327th GIR for its actions at Marvie, SE of Bastogne, in particular on December 20 and the night attack on December 23–24.

Opposite, below:
The Gen. 6th Armored, as George Hofmann writes in *The Super Sixth*, "entered the Battle of the Bulge by completing the relief of the 10th Armored" on December 26. Moving to Bastogne on the 28th, on New Year's Eve the division attacked through Bizory (as seen here), Mageret and Neffe. Heavy fighting and repeated German counterattacks were blunted by remarkable firepower from Div Arty who fired 53,045 rounds between January 1 and 7. This aerial view of Bizory shows 6th Armored on January 13.

Chapter 8

In honor of the members of the
327th GLIDER INFANTRY REGIMENT

who gave their life and paid their blood
in the defense of MARVIE during the German
winter offensive in December 1944.

En l'honneur des membres du
327th GLIDER INFANTRY REGIMENT
qui ont donné leur vie et versé leur sang
en défendant MARVIE durant la Bataille des Ardennes.

J A N U A R Y

END OF THE BULGE

AIRBORNE

HONOR AND COUNTRY

The Allies Counterattack

Below right:
Tanks of 712th Tk Bn, 90th Inf Div, the "Tough Ombres" crossed the Our on January 29, and would be instrumental in breaking through the Siegfried Line in February.

Bottom right:
An aerial view showing armor and infantry of the 6th Armored Division advancing through the snow, January 13.

Inset:
Memorial in honor of the 6th Armored's role in the Battle of the Bulge in Heinerscheid, Lux. *Traces of War*

Opposite, above:
Map of the campaign at the U.S. cemetery, Hamm.

Opposite, below:
Noville after liberation.

THE BATTLE DIDN'T end with the arrival of the new year. The Germans fought hard to reinvigorate their offensive, first with the attack on Allied airfields in the Low Countries—Operation *Bodenplatte*—then an offensive in Alsace (Operation *Nordwind*) intended to defeat Seventh Army and allow an attack on the unprotected rear of Third Army. Neither accomplished its goal and in early January the Allies attacked the "Bulge." It was slow progress, but Patton, as aggressive as ever, pushed on—with the 101st leading the way—first to a meeting with First Army at Houffalize in mid-January and then toward the Siegfried Line. The "Bulge" ceased to exist on January 25.

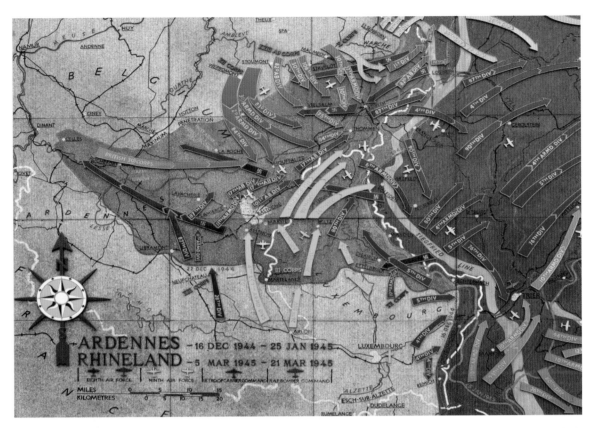

Houffalize was taken by 116th Panzer Division on December 19 but this Panther G, original turret number 111 now marked 401, probably from 1./16.Pz Regt, was knocked out later as the First and Third Armies fought to reduce the "Bulge." Local accounts suggest it was toppled into the river as a result of bombing and that the crew died as a result. The Panther was recovered from the Ourthe by engineers on September 20, 1948, and has been moved up the hill to become a memorial, as the modern photos show.

Opposite, Below:
84th Inf Div of First Army meets 11th Armd of Third Army in Houffalize on January 16. The Battle of the Bulge is almost over: the invasion of Germany is about to begin.

The Air Dimension

Above:
Operation Repulse—the resupply of 101st Airborne in Bastogne—was not without danger. Heavy flak led to a number of losses. In this case, *Ain't Misbehavin'* crash-landed successfully near Savy.

Right:
The bad weather meant that the Allies were unable to call on close support aircraft, but equally important was the absence of Photo Recon material. When the weather cleared, PR resumed immediately and this photo shows graphically how useful it was. This is Mont, just north of Houffalize, on December 26, as taken by 16th PR Sqn, RAF, part of the Strategic Reconnaissance Wing of the 2TAF. A high-altitude PR squadron, it was based at RAF Blackbushe and equipped with Spitfire PR Mk XIs which could, in an emergency, climb to 44,000ft (13,000m). It could carry vertically mounted cameras behind the cockpit or vertically oriented cameras under the wings.

Opposite, below:
Operation Repulse aircraft pass over Third Army—in the form of an M16 of 4th Armored's 489th AAA Automatic Weapons Bn.

Left:
Men of B Co, 506th PIR retrieve an A-4 Aerial Delivery Container full of medical supplies.

Below:
When available through the weather breaks, the close support of XIX Tactical Air Force was invaluable to Third Army.

Mardasson

THE BATTLE OF the Bulge was the largest, most costly battle fought by the U.S. Army in World War II, and its key was held at the small, crossroads town of Bastogne. There a few ad hoc units, from lightly armed paratroopers to vastly outnumbered tank, artillery and engineer battalions, held out alone against the might of a German Panzer Army for over 10 days, allowing time for full Allied strength to come to bear.

As such, the gallant stand at Bastogne has been commemorated by Americans and Belgians alike, beginning with the Mardassan Memorial, founded on July 4, 1946 with the participation of President Truman. The Memorial is shaped to represent the star of freedom, with five points, each measuring 100 feet high.

Along the crown are the names of the U.S. states, above paintings and engravings detailing the struggle, while the site provides a panoramic view of the ground so ferociously fought over during the siege.

Alongside the Memorial, having opened in time for the 70th anniversary of the battle, is the Bastogne War Museum with a variety of exhibits and interactive displays. In the town itself is the Bastogne Barracks, incorporating the basement in which the famous American decline to surrender—"Nuts!"—was written, with an immense exhibit across the street containing over 60 wartime vehicles from both combatants.

Above right photo: Marc Ryckaert/WikiCommons (CC BY 3.0)

Cemeteries

1 The Henri-Chapelle American Cemetery and Memorial contains the graves of 7,992 U.S. servicemen. There is also the Ardennes American Cemetery and Memorial at Neupré in Belgium which has 5,329 graves. *Romaine/WikiCommons (CC0)*

2 The German cemetery in the area of Bastogne is at Recogne, originally a cemetery for both U.S. and Germans, it has the graves of 6,807 German soldiers. *Pierre Bollen/WikiCommons (CC BY-SA 3.0)*

3 and 4 The Luxembourg American Cemetery and Memorial at Hamm is the main location for Bastogne burials. Also buried there—with his men—is Gen. Patton.

5 Memorial at the site of the temporary cemetery for the dead of the Battle of the Bulge at Foy. At one point nearly 3,000 men were buried there; most were reburied at Hamm. *Steve Hoar Photography*

6 Men of the 3042nd Graves Registration Company collect Allied and enemy dead just outside Bastogne, January 16, 1945.

GEORGE S. PATTON JR
GENERAL THIRD ARMY
CALIFORNIA DEC 21 1945

Bibliography

Traces of War (http://en.tracesofwar.com) is a fount of knowledge about—memorials, fortifications, cemeteries, points of interest, awards: definitely worth checking out. The location of the Historical Route boards and M4 turrets around Bastogne came from research on this site.

Bando, Mark: *Vanguard of the Crusade: The 101st Airborne Division in World War II*; Heimdal, 2012.

Bergstrom, Christer: *The Ardennes 1944–1945*; Vaktel Förlag/Casemate, 2014.

Forty, George: *Patton's Third Army at War*; Casemate, 2015.

Hofmann, George F.: *The Super Sixth*; Battery Press, 2000.

Killblane, Richard E.: "World War II: Pathfinders Resupply 101st Airborne Division Troops in Bastogne"; *World War II* magazine (online retrieval), Sept 2003.

King, Martin, & Michael Collins: *The Tigers of Bastogne: Voices of the 10th Armored Division in the Battle of the Bulge*; Casemate, 2013.

Mitchell, Colonel Ralph M.: *The 101st Airborne Division's Defense of Bastogne*; Combat Studies Institute, 1987.

MacDonald, Charles B.: *US Army in WW2: ETO The Siegfried Line Campaign*; DoA, Washington DC, 1963.

McAuliffe Kenneth J., Jr: "The Story of the NUTS! reply"; https://www.army.mil/article/92856.

Pallud, Jean Paul: *Battle of the Bulge Then and Now*; After the Battle, 1984.

Rapport, L. and Northwood, A.: *Rendezvous with Destiny*; 101st AB Assn, 1948.

USAREUR: *Battle Book The Battle of the Bulge.*

https://www.med-dept.com: 326th-airborne-medical-company.

Key to Map Symbols

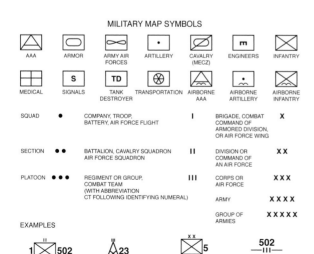

Battle of the Bulge Memorial dedicated on May 29, 2015. It is some 300m north of the 101st Airborne Memorial on the Foy–Bizory road at Jacques Wood.
Martin King